Dihedral

Mary-Jane Holmes

First Published in 2020
By Live Canon Poetry Ltd
www.livecanon.co.uk

All rights reserved

© Mary-Jane Holmes 2020

978-1-909703-70-4

The right of Mary-Jane Holmes to be identified as author of this work has been asserted by her in accordance with Section 77 of the Copyright, Design and Patents Act 1988.

A CIP catalogue record for this book is available from the British Library.

Dihedral

A Forward Prize nominee and Hawthornden Fellow, Mary-Jane has won the Bridport Poetry Prize, the Bath Novella-in-Flash Prize, the Martin Starkie Poetry Prize, Dromineer Fiction Prize, the Reflex Fiction and Mslexia Flash prize as well as the Bedford Poetry Competition. In 2020, she was shortlisted for the Beverley International Prize for Literature and longlisted for the UK National Poetry Prize. Mary-Jane's debut poetry collection *Heliotrope with Matches and Magnifying Glass* is published by Pindrop Press.

Her work appears in anthologies including *Best Small Fictions 2014/16/18* and *Best Microfictions* 2020 and in a variety of publications including *Magma, Mslexia, Modern Poetry in Translation, The Journal of Compressed Creative Arts, The Lonely Crowd*, and *Prole*.

She has an MA (Distinction) in Creative Writing from Kellogg College, Oxford and is currently studying for a PhD in poetry and translation at Newcastle University. Mary-Jane teaches courses and workshops on short fiction, microfiction, memoir, poetry and the novel.

Contents

Till the Rocks Melt wi' the Sun

Oh my love is like a red red.
Tyrian, Carmine, Mordant.
It is not Floribunda, Gallica,
Damask. It does not answer
to Chartreuse de Parme, Blaze
or Prince's Trust. No, my love
is casketed insects alum-boiled,
crushed seashells, rubbed deer
tails, the cap and hood of the King
Bolete. Oh my love is hydrogen
bonded and chained, dissolves
in chloroform, stains synovial
fluid. My love is an industrial
irritant, eats mucus membranes,
corrugates the lungs. My love
is the largest molecule ever found
in the universe. It smells of rasp-
berries, tastes of rum, resides
in a dust galaxy with propyl cyanide.

Dividing Line (after an instructional manual for American ranch owners to speak with their Mexican employees)

Today we will build a new
fence. First cut a right of way
thirty feet wide with an axe.

With a crowbar make holes ten
steps apart, one and a half feet
deep in rocks and two in dirt.

We want posts of pure heart;
white ones won't work.

When the posts are tight bring
the wire, the slick type for
putting dead men at the
corners.

Unroll it with this long bar and
pull the mesh tight. Wrap each
strand round the post, tie them
good. Stretch two of barbed
wire across the top. Nail it with
staples to each post.

If there is a hole below the net
you may put a rock or log
beneath but don't for one
moment think this'll keep love
penned, either in or out.

Hoy construimos una cerca nueva.
Primero, Vd. puede cortar un
sendero de treinta pies de ancha con
el hacha.

Entonces con las barras Vd. puede
hacer un pozo cada diez pazos.
Haga los pozos una y media pies de
hondo en piedra y dos en tierra.

Queremos postes de pura corazon;
los blancos no valen.

Cuando están apretados los postes,
traiga el amber. Necesitamos el
ambre liso para hacer hombre
muerto.

En las esquinas envolvemos el
alambre con este barra larga.
Apretamos muy fuerte este alambre
de tela. Dele vuelta cada raya al
poste y amárrelas bien. Entonces
apretamos dos rayas de alambre de
pico arriba. Clavamos el amber de
pico con grampas a cada poste.

Si hay un pozo abajo la tela Vd.
Puede poner una piedra o palo
abajo para ayudar a mantener. Las
cosas encerrado. Las cosas
encerrado.

Down the Long Long Line

Dark to light, the tunnel births the train and there's the river's head damned blue to reservoir, the ore rakes Da hushed lead from after the valley was drowned and the best sward spoiled, there's the clough where Ma netted sparrow (Spuggy, Sprog, Squidgie, Sparky) for a farthing a brace, there's the old hall where you went into service, steaming, pressing, goffering; lye burning the skin off your fingers, there's the hunting lodge where the master took you, holding his hand against your mouth while outside they beat and flushed grouse, there's the ginnel at the backend of town where they said you could be pure again: tansy oil, pennyroyal, rue, ergot, opium. There are the sidings where you lay wishing the wheels would roll your shame away, there's the train station where you marched the rails with the other girls: Lytton, Pankhurst, Kenney, Dunlop, with axe, stones and a message. *Deeds not Words*. There's the prison they put you in, there's the gag they prised open your jaw with, the tube they force fed you with, there is the spit you lobbied back, there's the polling card, the pen in your hand, there's the river's mouth cleaned up enough that fish (eelpout, cod, whiting, smelt) have taken to spawning again.

Dihedral

"Every photograph is a certificate of presence."
Roland Barthes, *Camera Lucida*

After the paramedics claimed the body, the coroner
his bundle of forms, my mother, untrained in grief's
protocol took a photo of where her husband died;
a kitchen in England tiled in scattered fossil and shell.
You can see where the tiler under-measured, the grout
line thick, jagged, not quite reaching the bespoke cabinets.

Six time zones back in another continent, before
the future vibrates as one incoming message, I'm lying
between resurrection fern and ocotillo, watching
the first sign of a desert spring. My body's outline -
a deviation of leaf-cutter ants on a caldera of limestone.
Turkey vultures kettle the bluff of our six-month rental.

I long for one of them to break its spiral, swoop in so close
I'll glimpse the pink scald of its head, but they rock
and soar, diffident in their teetering flight, knowing
the difference between living and dead, while I search
in every pixel for my father's presence, finding only
my mother's thumb blurring the lens with its raw imprint.

The Fall

After Robert Hass

Walking the chapel trail, I am content
to name things and not to think

crab apple, chaffinch,
gravedigger, e-bike.

Up ahead, the sign says
River Walk Closed.
Steep Drop.
But everyone knows

all women are masochists

so I delve
        into pestled mud, the mortared roots
        of wych-elm the size of ox's shin bones

and consider Ammon's Eve feeding
rovings with delicate fingers
                from distaff to spindle

the makings of supper at her feet,
the fire a roar of anticipation
                    for the pot.

This was how I was taught
to see myself
in love.

Task over condiment.

Tea on the table
at six o'clock, socks

darned, shirts
starched, folded.

That's where the path becomes
landslide, the fall
baroque - carmine water,
craquelure of stone on skin
and everything carried
to this point in ruins

– book, phone, this body –

a state of… what…

agony, egress, a desire
to prolong the petrichor
of blood, the aftertaste
of plush-lined rocks?

Above, peregrines cry
            'yield, yield'
and somewhere
in a turret dressed
in pink ashlar,

someone else will think
to place a vase of sweet peas
            on a windowsill,
                turn on
a lamp in an attic room
to better thread a needle.

What I Remembered on my Way to Buy Gin at Tesco Express

I took the path where the hedge was laid
but hadn't set. In the fields, ploughs
upturned Petalware and Spode, porcelain
my grandmother once kept behind veneer
and glass cabinets so our childish hands
wouldn't touch it. Not that we were interested
we had Witch's Hats and homemade swings,
the woods, the towpath where running home
for tea, I met a man in a trench coat
which he flashed open just long enough
for me to see what hid beneath it and feel
something burn inside as blue as his eyes
and more ceramic than any willow pattern
with its glazed elopers transformed into doves.

The Waiting Room

"On this island, there are trees that bear fruit like women, with shapes, bodies, eyes, hands, feet, hair, breasts, and vulvas like the vulvas of women. They are the most beautiful of face and hang by their hair…when they feel the wind and sun, they yell, 'Wāq Wāq, [help help] until their hair tears apart. When their hair tears, they die."

Ibn al-Wardi (d. 1348 ce)

We sit - an atoll of women – gently
metastasizing like slow-to-ripen fruit
beneath the strip-lighted pulse
of this wave-filled coast, archipelago
of scan, x-ray, magnetic resonance.

In this forest's bloom, we wait, hollow
as calabash, thumbing mounds of Vogue
and other *fabulas* of paradise that recount
little of how to stem lava flows or build
boats out of small pieces of wood.

The world flits around us in coral scrubs
and Crocs, exotic birds singing out
our names, our date of birth, clocking
our descent in cubits of hair length
while we learn what it is to be marooned,

to forever button, unbutton our clothes
until we are just a back-lit negative of trees
shadows on a chart, sum of our disposable
parts: stroma, lobule, areole, ovary, bone,
lymph, breath, wind, sun, the roar of a full moon.

Gazelle

For months he brought Impala irises, called her
his houri-eyed gazelle, asked if she'd go with him
up to the high pasture now the rains had come.
She sighed, searched for fresh vases, told him
his words were pure madness until that first
reluctant kiss amongst the flush of sorghum
where she felt her liver flatten to make room
for speed, smelt the musk of muscle flense air.

She broke her stride at the bend in the wadi,
looked up to find him, furlongs away, a speck
of dark beneath the Arak tree. He was right—
her flanks cut a lean curve, her mouth a muzzle
of velvet. She trotted back to where he stood,
bouquet still in hand stretched towards her, so
sweet she ate it as she pinned him to a low branch
with the bony nubs of her newly sprouted horns.

'Thirty-Six questions That Lead to Love' *(New York Times,* **2011***)* **as responded to by a selection of named and anonymous Andalusian female poets from the 8ᵗʰ to the 15ᵗʰ Century**

1.   Given the choice of anyone in the world, whom would you want as a dinner guest?

        I have hidden
        the name in a poem
        like treasure slipped
        between the folds of a hem

2.   Would you like to be famous? In what way?

        I am not one for cages. I am
        a lioness; why should I answer
        to dogs when I am deaf
        to the calls of lions?

3.   Before making a telephone call, do you ever rehearse what you are going to say? Why?

        What should I do mother?
        Tell me mother what should I do?
        What should I do?
        Mother tell me what should I do?
        What should I do? What will become of me?

4.   What would constitute a "perfect" day for you?

        A Sunday, its night pearled, no chaperone
        in sight and our bodies entwined
        like the sun in the arms of the moon,
        a gazelle in the clasp of a lion

5.   When did you last sing to yourself? To someone else?

How many of us have sung this to our mothers?
This madness must stop or I will die.
Somehow I must heal, fetch wine.

6.   If you were able to live to the age of 90 and retain either the mind or body of a 30- year-old for the last 60 years of your life, which would you want?

What hope is there
turned cobweb
like a toddler
with chains

for a woman, her body
who totters
or a slave laden
looking for her cane?

7.   Do you have a secret hunch about how you will die?

He is ready to kill if I venture outside.
I see it in the burn of his gait, his eyes.

8.   Name three things you and your partner appear to have in common.

Like you, my eyes
are dark, I am lonely
without friends

9.   For what in your life do you feel most grateful?

My garden at dawn, reeds
dew-strung like pendants
fluttering in the wind's palm

10.   If you could change anything about the way you were raised, what would it be?

Befriend strangers and foreigners, shun all
kinsfolk, they are as predatory as scorpions.

11. Take four minutes and tell your partner your life story in
as much detail as possible.

    Princess
            Spoil of war
                    Slave
                        Concubine
                            Wife
                                Poet

12. If you could wake up tomorrow having gained any one quality
or ability, what would it be?

    Forgiveness is the most beautiful thing when you have the
    power to bestow it

13. If a crystal ball could tell you the truth about yourself, your
life, the future or anything else, what would you want to know?

    Who can hide the day?

14. Is there something that you've dreamed of doing for a long time?
Why haven't you done it?

    If passion and song weren't ruined by wine
    I'd mix a cocktail of liquor, music, love,
    and drink and drink and drink

15. What is the greatest accomplishment of your life?

    Do you know of a better woman?

16. What do you value most in a friendship?

    You ignore my failings
    I won't mention your flaws

17. What is your most treasured memory?

That time together in the mountains,
a raven skimmed the crags and scars
so close to us I knew it was time
to welcome in your dark gloss of youth

18. What is your most terrible memory?

I dressed in black
to mourn his murder
only to be threatened
with the same sword

19. If you knew that in one year you would die suddenly, would
you change anything about the way you are now living? Why?

No longer fear the censor (the spy, the chaperone)
Shed tears only to carve a path to you.

20. What does friendship mean to you?

In its absence, the thirst of solitude

21. What roles do love and affection play in your life?

Just as the sun lights up the moon,
how easily it might also eclipse it

22. Alternate sharing something you consider a positive characteristic
of your partner.

Noble
    Virtuous
        Eloquent
            Wittol

23.　　How close and warm is your family?

Ｔhe young are prudent as their elders, yet
in battle, the elders are young as their progeny

24.　　How do you feel about your relationship with your mother?

How many of us have sung this to our mothers?
This madness must stop or I will die.
Somehow I must heal, fetch wine.

25.　　Make several true "we" statements each.

Him:

Remember that night we hid
amongst the scent of carnations,
the call of turtledoves, how
the myrtle leant its star-shadow
to the stream and the garden,
elated, bore testament to our love?

Her:

I remember what we did, how
indifferent the garden was, its claw
of undergrowth, birds chittering
of sorrow. The stream? A runnel.
What trees? What shadow – the stars?
Hah! Sent there only to spy on us.

26.　　Complete this sentence: "I wish I had someone with whom I
could share..."

... how lost I feel, as youth slips by
I see the orchard, ripe for the picking
yet no-one reaching for its harvest

27.   If you were going to become a close friend with your partner, please share what would be important for him or her to know.

        I follow my own path, offer my unadorned cheek
        to whomever I please, kiss those I hanker for

28.   Tell your partner what you like about them; be very honest this time, saying things that you might not say to someone you've just met.

        I want you to lift my ankle bracelets so they touch my earrings.

29.   Share with your partner an embarrassing moment in your life.

        You took up with a lesser woman,
        discarded the fruit-laden
        branch for a pollarded twig,
        left the orbit of the moon,
        for some shady constellation

30.   When did you last cry in front of another person? By yourself?

        These tears carry secrets like a river
        carves space in a garden, a garden
        makes space for a river. Undone,
        your hair flows loose about your face,
        a moon in the darkest hour as if dawn
        has lost a brother and from now on
        will wear nothing but mourning dress

31.   Tell your partner something that you like about them already.

        Your lips are a watercolour.

32.   What, if anything, is too serious to be joked about?

When I say it I mean it. Leave me alone.
Don't make me say it twice. My clothes
are torn, my necklace scattered.

33.   If you were to die this evening with no opportunity to
communicate with anyone, what would you most regret not
having told someone? Why haven't you told them yet?

            Surely we can be together again?
I have spent the embers of winter
          waiting at the appointed hour
but the nights pass and patience
          only tightens these shackles.

Wherever you are, I hope the land
          is well-watered; your new
country rich and abundant

34.   Your house, containing everything you own, catches fire.
After saving your loved ones and pets, you have time to safely
make a final dash to save any one item. What would it be? Why?

My plumes, paper, ink well

35.   Of all the people in your family, whose death would you find
most disturbing? Why?

How many of us have sung this to our mothers?

36.   Share a personal problem and ask your partner's advice on
how he or she might handle it.

Her: Shall I come to you or will you come to me?
Him: The garden needn't uproot itself, let in the breeze,
feel its faint breath.

Autophagia or What My Mother Did Once She Forgot

Absurd to think she was doing it on purpose
but I saw how she slipped slim between
the pleats of the sofa to forage amongst
the doctor's instructions: *A watch and a ruler:*
describe the difference. What year is this?
Copy this picture. Copy this picture:
my mother sharpening her one good incisor
as she lays out her options like morsels
of some Sunday dinner from the ration years:
tongue, brawn, knuckle, chitterlings.

Knuckle it is. Even the doctor is impressed
at how the tendon ribbons from its socket
so cleanly but now there is no stopping her—
The correct answer? Feed the famine intent
on consuming her so like Erysichthon
of Thessaly she devours herself
and I become her Mestra, shape-shifter sold
to dryad regiments of carers as the lollipop
lady or the wife of the peripatetic chiropodist
or the bitch that must've kidnapped her daughter.

She becomes smaller and smaller, until one day
all that is left is a small heart set to auto-defrost
in the microwave – turning, turning
on its bed of Pyrex, caramelizing the edges
that differentiate between time and distance.

The Lapidarist

While I was dreaming of dormant children
in dark woods red-breasted passerines
the thermal resistance of leaves
she was moving into my heart
with bow saws, lathes and copper drills.

I felt the acid bite of her in my blood, her spittle wetted
against the grit of emery abrading
every systolic and diastolic facet smooth
and yes now you mention it, it hurt
to hear my pulse ground to a *cuaderna via*

of agate, amethyst, onyx, sard and yet without
that viscera of sound, I am left abandoned, cold: an
intaglio of grand but empty summer pavilions and
forever upstretched palms.

Trip Advisor

Dear Guest,

It was a pleasure to be your host and hope you'll leave a five-star review taking into account all the little extra touches:

the cruelty-free shampoo, the fair-trade coffee, the make-up wipes

I notice you didn't use so now I see every pillowcase, facecloth, sheet is a Turin shroud of bronzer, eyeshadow, liquid lash

(Removal tip: a cotton ball scrape and witch hazel soak).

And all those chartreuse bitemarks on the bathmat?

(Removal tip: kitchen paper, patience, surgical spirit)

And the oat seed décolletage hard-pressed into the blanket?

(Removal tip: bicarbonate of soda, a soft-bristled brush).

And the blood, all that blood - a starburst of galaxies across the curtains.

(Removal tip: meat tenderizer, aspirin, a dash of lemon juice)

Dear guest…dearest – this is no way to make your mark – please check out of his mess at your earliest convenience

(Removal-tip –pack up your suitcase, apply concealer lightly on the tenderest places if you must: coral over purple, orange over black).

The management wishes you a safe and happy journey from here on out.

Good Luck

Somewhere

a man   sits in a field of ragweed, phone in hand

a woman   stands where the river doubles back on itself

a child   eats in a room with a misaligned ceiling rose

a fox   breaks cover from a topiary of yews

Climacterium

"Menopause is the return to where you were before."
Sandra Tsing Loh

Rain sits in her kitchen, resting her fog-heart in the kettle's steaming whistle. Manatees circle her ankles, left in the wake of Storm Ali or Bronagh or Doris (—now that was a girls' night out; she was standing water for days.) She throws them rainbows which they dive at, barrel-rolling for more, but she has no energy for games - her fingers feel like dry creek beds, her wrists have turned to rust. Outside, Sun burns up the harvest, farmers bray at her door with rakes, making the manatees moan like mermaids. *Oh to be an ocean again* she thinks, *to feel the pull of the moontide.* But there's little swell to her now, her bones crepitate like a heath fire. She turns on the fan, closes her eyes, condenses the white noise of blades to the sound of melting glaciers.

Stream of Consciousness in Self Isolation

Outside my window, a palimpsest of snow, moles
home-school their children in the art of house-building,
arctic terns drone the moors and one unidentified wader
sits on a capstone scoping for worms. Not a common snipe
or oyster catcher - my usual neighbours. Who was it recently
twittered 'our neighbours have been cancelled?' Bigger,
chevron-winged, cryptic brown and black. I've looked it up
dismissed dunlin, dotterel, sanderling, redshank … a woodcock?
Perhaps - but in a land devoid of trees? Perhaps - in a world gone
mad but in this *ménage rustique of sociability and solitude*
the imagination soars for something more exotic – a long-billed
dowitcher from Siberia, a rostratula from Africa, a tutukiwi
from New Zealand. Not that last one - it needs to be extant.
That word has so much more heft now doesn't it? I'll plump
for the dowitcher. My father (no longer extant) worked
in a brewery in Novosibirsk. I wonder if he ever saw a dowitcher
feeding on the banks of the Ob? All I know is he flew there
every month with an airline called Crash – but oh to fly
the longing for it, to be lifted out of all this, to be like the clocks,
to spring forward into the dogs days of a summer, salad days
unvaried except by accident. Salad - I've ordered Cut-
and-Come-Again and early seed potatoes that I'll chit and bury
in the soil left by the mole's excavations, like my grandparents did,
'earthing up' their Casablancas and Maris Pipers in another time
of crisis and now the sun still seemingly in its winter quarantine,
marches its slow gait across the horizon, appearing suddenly, luminous
as fever, above Goldsborough's cap of gritstone, over the Herdwicks
and Swaledales self-shielding from the three day north-easterly the Met
Office had predicted. Oh, to be able to forecast, to grasp some reassurance
from our modern-day oracles! What would Pythia make of our modelling
and algorithms? If we burn laurel and barley, pour cold water over a goat
to see if it shudders, would Apollo tell us what is to be done, or perhaps
his son Asclepius, god of medicine or perhaps his goddess granddaughters?
Hygeia, Panacea. Goddess. God. Godwit, that is what that bird is perched
on the wall, once thought of as 'the daintiest dish in England', its eggs
a trophy for any Victorian collector's display cabinet. The eggs I will go

and collect are from a more sustainable source – pure-breed Marans -
left by the farmer down the road in a small metal tin, each dozen with a happy
face felt-penned on its box and I will leave my money sprayed with a 3:1
mixture of surgical spirit and water in return, like the villagers once did
four miles from here in the Great Plague of 1636, where they picked up
fresh produce and left their money in vinegar in the single cup mark
set in the weathered rock that came to be known as the Butter Stone. Oh!
the bird has flown now, watch the worms come out of lockdown.

On Meeting a Coyote

Different from the time, sick
with vertigo I woke in dew
amongst fetlocked tongues
of roe deer, this mouth
corrals the fusiform hunger
of a wolf moon, yet
there is asylum in the eye
of the moment, an ossicle
of pause between *prey*
and *bolt*, the barbs of mesquite,
and if I walked my skin back
to its bone - to fur, to incisor,
to the call of oestrus, perhaps
there'd be a future in this chance
meeting, after all we both know
what it is to be tired of the cold,
to steal, to lie, the hysteria
of laughter in unknown territory
but tricksters that we are, we seek
sly exit back to what we know:
the patrol, the claw,
the dizzying tympany of the howl.

The First Stage of Love

Before the seed pod falls
        from the stem of the rose,

the thorn unstitches
        the spleen,

a fratch of wind blows
        through heath-rush,

hollows of hare scrapes, lifts
        the nests of birds

from trees, then whips, whips
        across valleys, deserts,

seas, only to return gritted
        with a kist of breath,

warm as the Calima, to bed
        our finite, air-filled hearts in.

LIVE CANON